It's a magic carpet ride.
Every door will open wide
To happy people like you.
What a beautiful
Sunny day
Sweepin' the clouds away,
On my way to where the air is sweet.

Can you tell me how to get,
How to get to Sesame Street?

The SONGS of SESAME STREET in POEMS and PICTURES

by Jeffrey Moss and
David Axlerod, Tony Geiss, Bruce Hart,
Emily Perl Kingsley, and Jon Stone

Illustrated by Normand Chartier

Featuring Jim Henson's Sesame Street Muppets

Random House / Children's Television Workshop

Lyrics copyright by Sesame Street, Inc. Lyrics by David Axlerod: "Fur," © 1975; "That Furry Blue Mommy of Mine," © 1977. Lyrics by David Axlerod and Emily Perl Kingsley: "Counting Is Wonderful," © 1975. Lyrics by Tony Geiss: "Imagination and You," © 1979; "In My Coloring Book," © 1980; "Lullaby But Not Good Night," © 1980; "Member of the Library," © 1980; "My Street," © 1977; "Proud to Be a Cow," © 1981; "Questions, Questions," © 1980; "Wonderful Me," © 1976. Lyrics by Emily Perl Kingsley: "I Still Love Him," © 1978; "When I Was Little," © 1974. Lyrics by Jon Stone and Bruce Hart: "Sesame Street Theme Song," © 1969.

Lyrics copyright by Festival Attractions, Inc. Lyrics by Jeffrey Moss: "Everyone Makes Mistakes," © 1970; "Goin' for a Ride," © 1969; "The Grouch Song," © 1970; "I Love Trash," © 1970; "People in Your Neighborhood," © 1969; "Rubber Duckie," © 1970; "Special," © 1970; "Up and Down," © 1970; "What Do I Do When I'm Alone?" © 1971.

Lyrics copyright by Backfin Music Co. Lyrics by Jeffrey Moss: "Still We Like Each Other," © 1972; "Ten Cookies," © 1977; "When Will My Birthday Come?" © 1977; "You Are My Neighbor," © 1978.

All compositions ASCAP

Library of Congress Cataloging in Publication Data: Main entry under title: The Songs of Sesame Street in poems and pictures. SUMMARY: Includes the words, without music, to songs from the popular television show. 1. Children's songs—United States—Texts. [1. Songs. 2. Puppets] I. Moss, Jeffrey. II. Children's Television Workshop. III. Sesame Street (Television program) PZ8.3.S7 1983 784.6'2405 83-3329 ISBN: 0-394-85245-1 (trade); 0-394-95245-6 (lib. bdg.)

Manufactured in the United States of America   1 2 3 4 5 6 7 8 9 0

Contents

People in Your Neighborhood

Oh, who are the people in your neighborhood,
In your neighborhood, in your neighborhood,
Oh, who are the people in your neighborhood,
The people who you meet each day?

Oh, the garbage man works hard each day.
He'll always take your trash away.
"I drive the biggest truck you've ever seen
And I'll make sure your streets are clean."

Oh, a bus driver works hard, you know,
To take you where you want to go.
"So if by chance you're going my way,
I'll see you on my bus one day."

Oh, the postman always brings the mail
Through rain or snow or sleet or hail.
"I'll work and work the whole day through
To get your letters safe to you."

Oh, a fireman is brave, it's said.
His engine is a shiny red.
"If there's a fire anywhere about
Well, I'll be sure to put it out."

Oh, who are the people in your neighborhood,
In your neighborhood, in your neighborhood,
Oh, who are the people in your neighborhood?
They're the people that you meet
When you're walking down the street,
They're the people who you meet each day.

MAIN ST.

OAK ST.

Rubber Duckie

Rubber Duckie, you're the one,
You make bath time lots of fun.
Rubber Duckie, I'm awfully fond of you,
Vo-Vo-Dee-O.

Rubber Duckie, joy of joys,
When I squeeze you, you make noise.
Rubber Duckie, you're my very best friend,
      it's true.

Oh, every day when I make my way to the tubby,
I find a little fellow who's cute and yellow and chubby,
Rub-a-Dub-Dubby.

Rubber Duckie, you're so fine
And I'm lucky that you're mine.
Rubber Duckie, I'm awfully fond of,
Rubber Duckie, I'd like a whole pond of,
Rubber Duckie, I'm awfully fond of you!

Lullaby But Not Good Night

Go to sleep, buddy Bert,
In your flannel nightshirt.
Happy dreams fill your head
As you snuggle down to bed.
Hushabye, get some rest
Like a pigeon in his nest.
Hushabye, get some rest
Like a pigeon in his nest.

I Love Trash

Oh, I love trash,
Anything dirty or dingy or dusty,
Anything ragged or rotten or rusty,
Oh, I love trash!

I have here a sneaker that's tattered and worn,
It's all full of holes and the laces are torn—
A gift from my mother the day I was born.
I love it because it's trash!

Oh, I love trash,
Anything dirty or dingy or dusty,
Anything ragged or rotten or rusty,
Oh, I love trash!

I have here some newspaper thirteen months old,
I've wrapped fish inside it, it's smelly and cold,
But I wouldn't trade it for a big pot of gold.
I love it because it's trash!

I've a clock that won't work and an old telephone,
A broken umbrella, a rusty trombone,
And I am delighted to call them my own.
I love them because they're trash!

Oh, I love trash,
Anything dirty or dingy or dusty,
Anything ragged or rotten or rusty,
Yes, I love, I love,
I love trash!

Still We Like Each Other

I have fur that's blue and fuzzy.
You may not have fur that's blue and fuzzy—
Still we like each other.

I like gooey peanut butter.
You may not like gooey peanut butter—
Still we like each other.

We are friends, you and me,
And it doesn't matter what we look like
Or if sometimes we don't agree.

'Cause we are people who are different.
People can be very very different.
Still they like each other.

You have your looks and likes and I have mine—
Still we like each other fine.

Wonderful Me

Who looks exactly the way that I look?
Me!
When I am reading who's holding the book?
Me!
When I want dinner who always will feed me?
Who's always handy whenever I need me?
Me! Me! Wonderful me!

Who is at home when I sit on my nest?
Me!
Who wears no clothes but is beautifully dressed?
Me!
And if I wake up at night and I turn on the light
And I look in the mirror, hey, gee, guess who I see there?
Wonderful me!

Counting Is Wonderful

Counting is wonderful, counting is marvelous,
Counting's the best thing to do.
Counting is happiness, counting is ecstasy,
I love to count, don't you?

You can count when you're happy,
You can count when you're sad,
Or count when you're frightened,
Count when you're mad!

You can count when you're standing,
You can count when you're stooped,
Or count when you're sneezing,
Count when you're pooped!

Counting is wonderful, counting is marvelous,
Counting's terrific and how!
I am pleased to announce you can add up amounts
By the pound, by the ounce, it's the counting that counts.
Put some bounce in your life and start counting now,
Yes, start counting now!

Ten Cookies

Ten cookies looking mighty fine.
Cookie Monster eat one
And now there are nine.
Nine cookies where there used to be ten.
Wish that I could have ten cookies again!

Nine cookies sitting on a plate.
Cookie Monster eat one
And now there are eight.

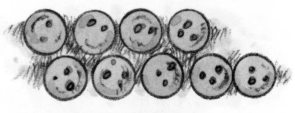

Eight cookies, not twenty or eleven.
Cookie Monster eat one
And now there are seven.

Seven cookies, now I do my tricks.
Cookie Monster eat one
And now there are six.

Six cookies, trouble is I've
Really got to eat one
And now there are five.

Five cookies, wish that there were more.
Cookie Monster eat one
Now there are just four.
Four cookies where there used to be ten.
Wish that I could have ten cookies again!

Four cookies pretty as can be.
Cookie Monster eat one
Now only three.

Three cookies, don't know what to do.
Cookie Monster eat one
And now just two.

Two cookies, to eat them would be fun.
Cookie Monster eat one
And now just one.

One cookie, one and only one.
Cookie Monster eat it
And now there are none.
No cookies where there used to be ten.
Wish that I could have ten cookies again!

Goin' for a Ride

Oh, I'm goin' for a ride,
Gonna sit behind the wheel,
Gonna drive along the road,
Oh, how happy I will feel.
And I'm gonna toot my horn,
Gonna travel near and far.
Yes, I'm goin' for a ride,
Goin' riding in a car.

And a car goes beep-beep!
And a car goes beep-beep!
Gonna travel near and far—
Goin' riding in a car.

Oh, I'm goin' for a ride
And I'm never coming back.
Gonna be an engineer,
Gonna speed along the track.
And you'll hear my whistle blow
And I'm happy to explain
That I'm goin' for a ride,
Goin' riding in a train.

And a train goes woohoo-wooo.
And a train goes woohoo-wooo.
And I'm happy to explain
I'm goin' riding in a train.

Oh, I'm goin' for a ride,
Gonna sail the ocean blue,
And I'm gonna be a captain
And I'm gonna have a crew.
Gonna sail the seven seas,
On the water I will float.
'Cause I'm goin' for a ride,
Goin' riding in a boat.

And a boat goes toot-toot!
And a boat goes toot-toot!
On the water I will float,
Goin' riding in a boat.

Yes, I'm goin' for a ride beep-beep!
Yes, I'm goin' for a ride woohoo-wooo!
Yes, I'm goin' for a ride toot-toot!
Yes, we're goin' for a ride!

Imagination and You

Just imagine you're in the sky.
Flap your arms,
You can fly.
What a view
From the blue
In your imagination.

Make believe that you're
In the sea.
What a fish
You can be—
Submarine or sardine
In your imagination.

You can be an astronaut
Searching for a star.
Drive a bus,
Be a car.
All you gotta do
Is make believe you are.

Be an elephant in the zoo,
Wave your trunk,
Look at you!
Be a king,
Be a clown,
Be a child, too.
All you need is imagination
And you.

In My Coloring Book

Purple sun,
Yellow sky,
Just for fun.
Don't ask why
I make the world all different
In my coloring book.
Apples blue,
Silver tree,
Wrong for you,
Right for me.
I'm playing Mother Nature
In my coloring book.
The sky gets boring
When it's always blue
So I'm exploring
Ways to make it new—
Orange brook,
Cow of green,
Don't they look
Really keen!
A crimson mountain is behind them
And there is just one place you'll find them . . .
In my coloring book.

What Do I Do When I'm Alone?

What do I do when I'm alone?
Well, sometimes I sing a little song.
La la la la la la—
That is the song I sing.

What do I do when I'm alone?
Well, sometimes I do a little dance.
I jump and I hop, hop, hop—
That is my little dance.

And sometimes when I'm all alone,
I pretend that I can fly.
And I touch all the clouds
And I wave to the birds as they pass by.

But sometimes when I am all alone,
Well, sometimes I feel a little sad.
'Cause there's no one to share my song,
No one to fly with me.

So sometimes when I am all alone
I think of how happy I would be
If I weren't alone
And you were here with me.

The Grouch Song

If you wake up in the morning mean and grumpy
And you frown at everybody that you see,
If you like your oatmeal nice and cold and lumpy—
Then you're a grouch like me!

If you love it when it's wet and cold and raining
And the music that you like is all off-key,
If you're happiest whenever you're complaining—
Then you're a grouch like me!

If you hate it when your grandma kisses you,
You know what? Well, me too!
If you love to watch a garbage truck roll by,
You know what? So do I!

And if you think a great big pile of trash is pretty
And that ice cream is as yucchy as can be,
If you cannot stand a cuddly little kitty—
Then you're a grouch like me!

Special

Nobody's eyes are quite the same as your eyes.
Some eyes are brown and some are big and blue.
But your eyes are special just because they're your eyes
And you are special just because you're you.

Nobody's voice sounds quite the same as your voice.
Singing or laughing or calling out my name.
Your voice is special just because it's your voice.
Nobody's voice sounds quite the same.

You're somebody special, there's nobody like you.
You won't find another if you travel far and wide.
You've got your own special feelings, your own special secrets,
Your own special happiness deep inside.

And nobody's smile is quite the same as your smile,
Nobody can smile just the way you do.
Your smile is special just because it's your smile
And you are special just because you're you.

You're the one and the only, extraordinary
Very special you!

29

Up and Down

Oh, I look up and see a birdie flying high and free.
Well, I look down and then the sidewalk is what I see.
I look up and see the sky,
I look down and see the ground,
I look at you and sing a song about up and down.

Oh, I look up and see an airplane flying, yes, I do!
I look down and see my foot and then I see my shoe!
I look up and see the sky,
I look down and see the ground,
I look at you and sing a song about up and down.

Oh, I look up and see the ceiling and there's one thing more,
I look down and see the rug and then I see the floor.
I look up and see the sky,
I look down and see the ground,
I look at you and sing a song about up and down!
Up and down! Up and down!

Fur

Fur! I am covered with fur
From my snoot to my spur,
I'm a furry fellow.
Fur! When you stroke it I purr,
When you poke it I grrr.
It's maroon and yellow.
Fur! Keeps me warm when it's brrr.
Don't you wish that you were fairly bursting with
Fur, fur, fur?
Yes, fur is beautiful, fur is clever,
Furthermore, I love fur furever.
Fur! Unfurgettable fur!

My Street

Hello, lamppost!
Hello, tree!
Hello, neighbor
Smiling at me!
I'm at home
And it's a treat
Walking down my street.

Hello, bus stop!
Hello, store!
Hello, steps
In front of my door!
Feeling good
'Cause life is sweet
Walking down my street.

I know every crack that's in the sidewalk.
I know where the street begins and ends.
I know all the windows on the houses,
Like the people in them, they're my friends.

Hello, mailbox!
Hello, car!
Hello, friends,
Wherever you are!

I just hope
Someday we meet
Walking down
My street!

You Are My Neighbor

You are my neighbor, that's what you are.
From my house to your house is not very far.
If you need a favor, just knock on my door,
You're someone I'm happy to do a favor for.
You are my neighbor and I just want to say
I'd really miss you if you went away.
'Cause I'm a neighbor who feels lucky, yes, I do,
Having a neighbor nice as you.

You are my neighbor, that's what you are.
From my house to your house is not very far.
You're someone to talk to when I'm feeling glum,
Someone to borrow a cup of birdseed from.
You are my neighbor and I just want to say
I would feel awful if you moved away.
'Cause I'm a neighbor who feels lucky, yes, I do,
Having a neighbor nice as you.

When I Was Little

When I was little I used to be scared
of being alone in the night.
I'd pull the blankets up over my head
And pray that the sky would get light.

But then my mommy sat by my bed
And said there was nothing to fear,
'Cause nothing scary went on in the night
And she and my daddy were near.

When I was little I used to be scared
Of taking a bath in the tub.
I thought when the water ran down the drain
That I would go with it . . . glub-glub.

But my old buddy Bert said,
"Come on, use your brain.
If you just take a look, you will see
That you NEVER could fit
Through that very small drain!"
Now my tubby's where I love to be.

When Will My Birthday Come?

When will my birthday come?
When will my own day be?
Seems that there are so many days,
There must be a day for me.

When will my birthday come?
When will my friends be near?
Letting me know they care for me
And showing they're glad I'm here.

Will it come in spring?
Will it come in fall?
Sometimes I wonder if it will come at all.

When is my special day?
Sometimes I'm not too sure.
Will it be next November or maybe June?
When will my birthday come? I hope it's soon.

Member of the Library

I'm gonna get a cookbook
And learn to bake a pie.
I'm gonna get a flying book
To teach me how to fly.
I'm gonna get a garden book
And learn to plant a seed.
I'll also get a reading book
To teach me how to read.
I'm glad I know my numbers
And learned my ABC
'Cause now I am a member of the library!

Proud to Be a Cow

Sometimes when I'm in a moooooood
I think of animals I might have been.
I could have been a wombat or a goose,
I could have been a monkey or a moose,
I could have been a dragon,
Or a horse that pulls a wagon,
But I'm not.
So what!
Let others be a lion or a lamb,
I'm proud to be the creature that I am!
I'm proud, proud, proud to be a cow!

My skin is soft as silk,
I give a lot of milk,
I never pull a wagon or a plow.
I'm proud, proud, proud to be a cow!
I'm glad that I say "moo" and not "meow"!
My eyes are soft and dreamy,
My butter's rich and creamy,
I'm proud, proud, proud to be a cow!

I've horns upon my head,
A meadow is my bed,
I think that every cow should take a bow.
I'm proud, proud, proud to be a cow!
I'm glad that I say "moo" and not "bow-wow"!
I'm proud I have an udder
Like my father—no, my mudder!
I'm proud, proud, proud to be a cow!

Everyone Makes Mistakes

I've a special secret children ought to know,
It's about the little mistakes you make as you begin to grow.
If you make a mistake, you shouldn't start to cry,
Mistakes are not so bad and here is why:

Everyone makes mistakes, oh yes, they do.
Your sister and your brother and your dad and mother, too.
Big people, small people,
Matter of fact, all people.
Everyone makes mistakes, so why can't you?

If you make a mistake while counting up to ten,
Well, don't get mad and don't be sad, just start to count again.
And if you should only get to eight or nine,
I'm still your friend and I still like you fine.

If you spill a glass of milk all over the floor,
Well, your mom and dad'll still like you just as much as they did before.
'Cause when Mother and Dad were just as small as you,
I'll bet that they knocked their milk over, too.
'Cause . . .

Everyone makes mistakes, oh yes, they do.
Your sister and your brother and your dad and mother, too.
Big people, small people,
Matter of fact, all people.
Everyone makes mistakes, so why can't you?
If everyone in the whole wide world makes mistakes,
Then why can't you?

Questions, Questions

Why is the sky so blue?
What makes a person sneeze?
When is it half past two?
Who makes a dog have fleas?
Why is my head on top?
Why are my feet below?
What makes the popcorn pop?
What makes a glowworm glow?

Questions, questions,
Wanting to know,
Ask me, ask me
But take it slow.
Ask me Where? What?
When? Why?
But *if you rush
How can I reply*?

I Still Love Him

I don't love the pudding he dumped in my bed,
I don't love the airplane he threw at my head.
When he's acting like that, it just makes me see red!
But I still love him!

I don't love spaghetti inside my new shoes,
I don't love his drumming when I'm trying to snooze.
There surely are days when he gives me the blues,
But I still love him!

It's not that he's a menace,
He's just a little kid.
It's not that I don't love him,
I just don't love what he did!

I don't love the butter he spread on the chair,
I don't love the honey he poured in his hair.
He pulled all the stuffing from his new teddy bear,
But I still love him!

That Furry Blue Mommy of Mine

When day is ending
And shadows grow long,
Who waits at home
To sing me a song?
There's only one
Who makes me feel fine,
That furry blue mommy of mine!

When I am sick
Who makes sure I get well?
Who helps me learn
To read and to spell?
Both me and Daddy
Think she's divine,
That furry blue mommy of mine!

I see her face before me now,
So beautiful and shy,
As furry as a polar bear
And bluer than the sky.

Who cooks my dinner
And washes my sox?
Cute as a bug
And strong as an ox?

When I grow up
I'll build her a shrine,
That furry blue mommy,
Oh, I love you, Mommy,
That furry blue mommy of mine!

Sesame Street Theme

Sunny day
Sweepin' the clouds away,
On my way to where the air is sweet.

Can you tell me how to get,
How to get to Sesame Street?

Come and play,
Everything's A-okay.
Friendly neighbors there,
That's where we meet.

Can you tell me how to get,
How to get to Sesame Street?